✳
OUR SONG,
OUR TOIL

OUR SONG, OUR TOIL

THE STORY OF AMERICAN SLAVERY AS TOLD BY SLAVES

EDITED BY
MICHELE STEPTO

The Millbrook Press
Brookfield, Connecticut

Library of Congress Cataloging-in-Publication Data
Our song, our toil : the story of American slavery as told by slaves /
edited by Michele Stepto.
p.   cm.
Includes bibliographical references and index.
Summary: Recounts the story of American slavery from African
captivity to emancipation, through excerpts from slave
autobiographies and slavery documents.
ISBN 1-56294-401-0 (lib. bdg.)
1. Slaves—United States—Biography—Juvenile literature.
2. Slavery—United States—History—Juvenile literature.
[1. Slavery—History—Sources.]   I. Stepto, Michele.
E444.097   1994
973'.0496'00922—dc20   93-8323   CIP   AC

Published by The Millbrook Press
2 Old New Milford Road, Brookfield, Connecticut 06804

for Miguel and Maya,
John-Paul and Naomi

CONTENTS

Around us the history of the land has centred for thrice a hundred years; out of the nation's heart we have called all that was best to throttle and subdue all that was worst; fire and blood, prayer and sacrifice, have billowed over this people, and they have found peace only in the altars of the God of Right. Nor has our gift of the Spirit been merely passive. Actively we have woven ourselves with the very warp and woof of this nation,—we fought their battles, shared their sorrow, mingled our blood with theirs, and generation after generation have pleaded with a headstrong, careless people to despise not Justice, Mercy, and Truth, lest the nation be smitten with a curse. Our song, our toil, our cheer, and warning have been given to this nation in blood-brotherhood. Are not these gifts worth the giving? Is not this work and striving? Would America have been America without her Negro people?

W.E.B. Du Bois
The Souls of Black Folk
1903

OUR SONG,
OUR TOIL

INTRODUCTION

No one knows for certain when and where in North America Africans were first sold as slaves. We do know that in August of 1619, a Dutch ship carrying twenty Africans anchored at Jamestown, Virginia. This is the earliest record of captive Africans arriving in North America. Were the twenty persons on that ship sold as servants? Almost certainly. Were they sold into what we now call slavery? Probably not, since slavery did not exist in North America in 1619. The laws that would bring it into being had not yet been written.

Before 1640, servants in the North American colonies worked under indentures. An indenture was a work contract between master and servant. It stated how and for how long the servant would work for the master. It also stated what the servant would receive in return from the master, both during service and when the term of service ended. Indenture contracts guaranteed masters a stable work force. They also guaranteed that servants would have food, clothing, and shelter during the time they worked, and their own land or start-up money, or both, when the period of service ended.

Sometimes people were sold into indentured servitude as a punishment for crime. Sometimes people sold themselves into servitude as a way of acquiring money or land after a few years. In either case, their contracts specified how many years they were to serve. Most indentures lasted between four and seven years, although indentured children typically served until they were twenty-one. Indentured servants were often ill-treated, ill-clothed, ill-fed, and overworked. Even so, they could look forward to their freedom. Indentured servitude was in this way very different from slavery, which was for life.

Indentured servitude differed from slavery in another important way. It was not hereditary. When indentured servants had children, those children did not automatically become indentured servants. They were born free. People could, and often did, sell their children into servitude in order to raise money, but this required a new indenture contract.

In 1640 an important event took place. That year, in Virginia, three indentured servants ran away from their masters. One was a Dutchman, one was a Scot, and the third was an African named John Punch. The three were captured in Maryland and returned to their masters. As punishment, the Virginia court added an extra four years to the Dutchman's and the Scot's terms of service. But John Punch, the African, was ordered to serve his master "for the time of his natural life." As punishment for running away, John Punch—and only John Punch—was made a slave. It may be that other Africans were treated as slaves before John Punch, but he is the first person on record to be enslaved in North America.

In 1641, Massachusetts colony recognized slavery by law. The new law said that slavery was forbidden except in the case of "lawful captives taken in just wars" and "strangers . . . sold to us." This law did two things. It protected the liberty of the English settlers, and it allowed them to enslave others—Indians captured in war and African "strangers" sold to them by slave traders.

During the next hundred years, Connecticut, Virginia, Maryland, New York, New Jersey, South Carolina, Rhode Island, Pennsylvania, North Carolina, and Georgia all passed similar laws. One after another, the colonial assemblies of North America legalized slavery. They also passed dozens of laws governing the sale, use, and conduct of their new human "property." In 1705, Virginia gathered its many slave laws together into North America's first "slave code."

There was nothing natural about slavery. It was a social institution, put in place piece by legal piece. From the beginning, it applied only to people of color. Slavery allowed the white settlers to use the labor of Indian and African people without sharing the wealth that their labor created.

But as the years went by, only Africans and African Americans were enslaved. Why? Indians often died from smallpox and other Old World diseases. Many ran away, returning to their communities. Enslaved Africans also died from disease, but it was harder for them to run away. They did not know the land as well as Indians did, nor could they hide as easily. In the end, the white colonists found it easier to enslave Africans and their American-born children.

There were always English settlers who opposed slavery. But their numbers were small and they were always outvoted. The laws that created racial slavery in North America went into place. By 1700, these laws defined and enforced the enslavement *from birth* and *for life* of all children born to enslaved women. This meant most—though not all—African Americans.

How did Africans come to be enslaved so far from their homes? Before slavery began in the North American colonies, the Atlantic slave trade began. When Europeans first came to the Americas, they wanted a steady supply of cheap labor. They found it in West Africa.

These Europeans—especially the Portuguese at first—began taking West Africans from their homes and selling them into labor in the New World. By the time slavery was legalized in North America, the Atlantic slave trade was bringing Africans to the Americas by the millions.

Africans also took part in the Atlantic slave trade, although they were the chief victims of it. African slave traders brought captive men, women, and children from their inland towns and villages to the West African coast. There they traded them to the waiting Europeans in return for guns, cloth, whiskey, and other goods.

Most of the writers in this book—descendants of people first brought from West Africa to the Americas in the Atlantic slave trade—lived in the 1800s. Over the many years of enslavement, they and their kin had become Americans, and wrote of their enslavement, so that other Americans would listen and understand.

While slavery lasted, they wrote to move other Americans to anger and to action. When slavery was finally ended, they wrote to remind others of what enslaved Americans had gone through. In the long history of human slavery, no other people have left as complete and vivid a record of their enslavement as those once enslaved in the United States. Their words continue to teach us of the courage, dignity, and hope that people can show in the face of suffering.

The story of slavery is American history, and it is one of the most important stories that can ever be told in the United States. Whatever color we may be, wherever our families may have come from, as Americans we can all learn from it. Knowing our past, knowing how we have come to be who we are, we can enter the future with greater strength and understanding.

INTO CAPTIVITY

West Africans came to be taken captive in Africa in various ways. Most were prisoners of war who had been sold to slave traders. Some had been sold into slavery as punishment for a crime. Many were simply kidnapped, although such kidnapping was itself a crime.

COFFLES, BARRACOONS, AND MIDDLE PASSAGE

For most of the captives, the long trip to the Americas began with a forced march to the West African coast. Torn away from their homes, people were tied together in groups, called "coffles," and then herded overland. Sometimes the march took many months. Once they reached the coast, they might be held for weeks in the "barra-coons," or slave fort dungeons, waiting to be shipped. Next came the dread journey across the Atlantic Ocean, in the hold, or between the decks of a slave ship. This journey was called the "Middle Passage."

Slaves resisted their captors in Africa and at sea. Pictured in this painting by
Nathaniel Jocelyn is Cinqué, an African who led a mutiny aboard a Spanish
slave ship in 1839. When the ship was brought ashore in New London, Connecticut, Cinqué and other rebel slaves were tried for mutiny. In 1841, the
U.S. Supreme Court ruled that they had been enslaved illegally. Cinqué and
other mutineers returned to Africa that year.

One third of all the captives died along the way—on the forced march, in the barracoons, or during the Middle Passage. They died of infected wounds, of disease, of starvation, of hopelessness. Some committed suicide. At least 10 million West Africans were brought to the Americas during the years of the Atlantic slave trade. That means that at least 5 million more did not survive the trip. Of those who did survive, a half million were sold as slaves in what is now the United States.

Olaudah Equiano

Olaudah Equiano survived. He was born in 1745 in Benin, now a part of the West African nation of Nigeria. His mother and father were well-to-do members of a farming village.

One day, when Olaudah was eleven, he and his sister were kidnapped by slave traders. Many years later, Olaudah Equiano wrote about that day.

One day, when all our people were gone out to their works as usual, and only I and my dear sister were left to mind the house, two men and a woman got over our walls, and in a moment seized us both, and without giving us time to cry out, or make resistance, they *stopped our mouths,* and ran off with us into the nearest wood. Here they tied our hands, and continued to carry us as far as they could, till night came on, when we reached a small house, where the robbers halted for refreshment, and spent the night. We were then unbound, but were unable to take any food; and, being quite overpowered by fatigue and grief, our only relief was some sleep, which *allayed* our misfortune for a short time. The next morning we left the house, and continued travelling all the day. For a long time we

gagged us

made us forget

had kept [to] the woods, but at last we came into a road which I believed I knew. I had now some hopes of being *delivered;* for we had advanced but a little way before I discovered some people at a distance, on which I began to cry out for their assistance; but my cries had no other effect than to make them tie me faster and stop my mouth, and then they put me into a large sack. They also stopped my sister's mouth, and tied her hands; and in this manner we proceeded till we were out of sight of these people. When we went to rest the following night, they offered us some *victuals,* but we refused it; and the only comfort we had was in being in one another's arms all that night, and bathing each other with our tears. But alas! we were soon deprived of even the small comfort of weeping together. The next day proved a day of greater sorrow than I had yet experienced; for my sister and I were then separated, while we lay clasped in each other's arms. It was in vain that we *besought* them not to part us; she was torn from me. . . .

rescued

food

begged

The kidnappers sold Olaudah's sister to one person, and Olaudah to another. In the weeks that followed, he passed through the hands of many different owners. Each time Olaudah was sold, he was taken farther away from his home. Six months after he was kidnapped, Olaudah reached the West African coast and was put on board a slave ship. There he waited for several days, while the ship filled up with other slaves. Finally, the ship set sail.

The *stench* of the hold while we were on the coast was so intolerably *loathsome,* that it was dangerous to remain there for any time, and some of us had been permitted to stay on the deck for the fresh air; but now that the whole ship's cargo were confined together, it became absolutely *pestilential.* The closeness of the place, and the heat of the climate, added to the

bad smell
disgusting

unhealthy

number in the ship, which was so crowded that each had scarcely room to turn himself, almost suffocated us. This wretched situation was again *aggravated* by the *galling* of the chains, now became *insupportable,* and the filth of the *necessary tubs,* into which the children often fell, and were almost suffocated. The shrieks of the women, and the groans of the dying, *rendered* the whole a scene of horror almost inconceivable. Happily perhaps, for

worsened; rubbing
unbearable; toilets

made

Although they were valuable ''cargo,'' captives were abused during Middle Passage and sometimes even killed. In this engraving, an enslaver wields a sword threateningly in a ship's hold where two slaves have been whipped.

myself, I was soon reduced so low here that it was thought
necessary to keep me almost always on deck; and from my ex-
treme youth I was not put in *fetters*. In this situation I expected   *chains*
every hour to share the fate of my companions, some of whom
were almost daily brought upon deck at the point of death, which
I began to hope would soon put an end to my miseries. . . .
Every circumstance I met with, served only to render my state
more painful, and heightened my *apprehensions*, and my opin-   *fears*
ion of the cruelty of the whites.

    One day they had taken a number of fishes; and when they
had killed and satisfied themselves with as many as they thought
fit, to our astonishment who were on deck, rather than give any
of them to us to eat, as we expected, they tossed the remaining
fish into the sea again, although we begged and prayed for some
as well as we could, but in vain; and some of my countrymen,
being pressed by hunger, took *an opportunity*, when they thought   *a chance*
no one saw them, of trying to get a little *privately*; but they were   *secretly*
discovered, and the attempt *procured* them some very severe   *earned*
floggings. One day, when we had a smooth sea and moderate   *beatings*
wind, two of my wearied countrymen who were chained together (I was near them at the time), preferring death to such a
life of misery, somehow made through the nettings and jumped
into the sea; immediately, another quite *dejected* fellow, who, on   *hopeless*
account of his illness, was *suffered* to be out of *irons*, also fol-   *allowed; chains*
lowed their example; and I believe many more would very soon
have done the same, if they had not been prevented by the ship's
crew, who were instantly alarmed. Those of us that were the
most active, were in a moment put down under the deck; and
there was such a noise and confusion amongst the people of the
ship as I never heard before, to stop her, and get the boat out
to go after the slaves. However, two of the wretches were
drowned, but they got the other, and afterwards flogged him
unmercifully, for thus attempting to prefer death to slavery.

The slave ship took Olaudah to Virginia. There, he was sold to a British naval officer, who gave him a new name—Gustavus Vassa—and took him to England. After six years, he was sold again to a Philadelphia Quaker. From this man Olaudah bought his freedom at the age of twenty-one. He had been enslaved for ten years.

As a free man, Olaudah lived in London, where he worked as a barber and took part in the anti-slavery movement. In 1789, he told the story of his life in a book called *The Life of Olaudah Equiano, or Gustavus Vassa, the African, Written by Himself.*

"BORN A SLAVE"

Olaudah Equiano was enslaved in his West African homeland and brought to America in a slave ship. But most people enslaved in what is now the United States were born into slavery right here.

"I was born a slave; but I never knew it till six years of happy childhood had passed away." So Harriet Jacobs of North Carolina began her autobiography. Like so many men and women who wrote about their enslavement, Harriet Jacobs remembered what it was like to discover that she was a slave, to discover that she had indeed been "born a slave." But what does it mean to be "born a slave"?

SLAVERY AND MOTHERHOOD

Slavery in North America was based on the ancient law that "the child follows the condition of its mother." This meant that in determining who was a slave and who was free, only the mother's status or "condition" counted. The children of free women, including free

A woman and baby overlook a scene of slavery in this painting by Eastman Johnson. Although the painting shows that slave homes were poor, many point out that the reality of slavery was even worse: Many slave children never knew what it was like to have a home, since they could be separated from loved ones at any time.

African-American women, were born into freedom. But each and every child born to an enslaved woman was born a slave, even if its father was a free man.

An enslaved woman's master owned not only her, but also her children. He owned not only her living children, but those not yet born. And because he owned them, he could sell them. The enslaved woman was thus a different kind of "property" from the enslaved man. As both a laborer and a mother, she created enormous wealth for those who owned her.

This was especially important after 1808, when the slave trade to Africa was outlawed. Now captive Africans could no longer be legally imported and sold in the United States. At the same time, the regions that would become Alabama, Mississippi, and Louisiana were being settled. As the demand for labor on this frontier grew, slaveholding society looked to the enslaved woman to enlarge its work force with her children.

EARLY GOOD-BYES

Separations came early in an enslaved child's life. Most enslaved mothers had to return to work very soon after giving birth. Some would carry their babies into the fields with them. Some would leave them in the care of another slave or relative who was too old for hard labor. Sometimes free men and women raised the children of their enslaved kin.

It often happened that the enslaved mother and child did not see each other for many months. Even so, many enslaved children were well cared for and happy during their first years. But happy or sad, they were expected to begin working at an early age, and this often meant separation from people they loved. To be born a slave meant having to say good-bye at a young age.

Frederick Douglass

Frederick Douglass remembered seeing his mother only four or five times in his life. He was separated from her shortly after birth and sent to live with his grandparents, Betsey and Isaac Bailey. Betsey was owned by the same man who owned Frederick's mother and Frederick. Isaac was a free man. The Baileys lived in a cabin far from the center of a large Maryland plantation. In it, they took care of many of their grandchildren, including Frederick.

As the children grew older, one by one they were taken from the Baileys and brought to the plantation center to be raised as slaves. In *My Bondage and My Freedom,* Frederick Douglass wrote of his early years with his grandparents as happy ones. He also wrote of what it was like to discover that he would someday be taken from them.

Living here, with my dear old grandmother and grandfather, it was a long time before I knew myself to be a [slave]. I knew many other things before I knew that. Grandmother and grandfather were the greatest people in the world to me; and being with them so snugly in their own little cabin—I supposed it be their own—knowing no higher authority over me or the other children than the authority of grandmamma, for a time there was nothing to disturb me; but, as I grew larger and older, I learned by degrees the sad fact, that the "little hut," and the lot on which it stood, belonged not to my dear old grandparents, but to some person who lived a great distance off and who was called, by grandmother, "OLD MASTER." I further learned the sadder fact, that not only the house and lot, but that grandmother herself, (grandfather was free,) and all the little children around her, belonged to this mysterious *personage*, called by grandmother, with every mark of *reverence*, "Old Master." Thus early did clouds and shadows begin to fall upon my path. . . . I was told that this "old master," whose name seemed ever to be mentioned with fear and shuddering, only allowed the children to live with grandmother for a limited time, and that in fact as soon as they were big enough, they were promptly taken away, to live with the said "old master" . . . .

person

deep respect

I dreaded the thought of going to live with that mysterious "old master," whose name I never heard mentioned with affection, but always with fear. I look back to this as among the heaviest of my childhood's sorrows. My grandmother! my grandmother! and the little hut, and the joyous circle under her care, but especially [she], who made us sorry when she left us but for an hour, and glad on her return,—how could I leave her and the good old home?

Harriet Jacobs

Harriet Jacobs considered her early years in Edenton, North Carolina, especially fortunate. Her mother and father, Delilah and Daniel Jacobs, were owned by different masters, but they were allowed to live together and raise their two children, Harriet and William. Delilah Jacobs was a lady's maid. Daniel Jacobs was a highly skilled carpenter who was allowed by his master to hire out his time.

When Harriet was six, Delilah died, and Harriet was sent for to take her mother's place. It was then that she first learned she was a slave. In her autobiography, *Incidents in the Life of a Slave Girl,* Jacobs wrote of those early years.

I was told my home was now to be with [my mother's] mistress; and I found it a happy one. No *toilsome* or disagreeable duties were imposed upon me. My mistress was so kind to me that I was always glad to do *her bidding,* and proud to labor for her as much as my young years would permit. I would sit by her side for hours, sewing diligently, with a heart as free from care as that of any free-born white child. When she thought I was tired, she would send me out to run and jump; and away I bounded, to gather berries or flowers to decorate her room. Those were happy days—too happy to last. The slave child had no thought for the morrow; but there came that *blight,* which too surely waits on every human being born to be *a chattel.*

When I was nearly twelve years old, my kind mistress sickened and died. As I saw the cheek grow paler, and the eye more glassy, how earnestly I prayed in my heart that she might live! I loved her; for she had been almost like a mother to me. My prayers were not answered. She died, and they buried her in the little churchyard, where, day after day, my tears fell upon her grave.

I was sent to spend a week with my grandmother. I was now old enough to begin to think of the future; and again and again I asked myself what they would do with me. I felt sure I should never find another mistress so kind as the one who was gone. She had promised my dying mother that her children should never suffer for any thing; and when I remembered that, and recalled her many proofs of attachment to me, I could not help having some hopes that she had left me free. My friends were almost certain it would be so. They thought she would be sure to do it, on account of my mother's love and faithful service. But, alas! we all know that the memory of a faithful slave does not *avail* much to save her children from the auction block.

After a brief period of suspense, the will of my mistress was read, and we learned that she had *bequeathed* me to her sister's

tiring

what she asked

curse
property

count for

given

me or to which I may be in any manner entitled. And I hereby nominate
and appoint my friend Doct James
Norcom Executor of this my last
will and testament. In testimony
of which I have hereunto Set my
hand and Seal, the eighth Day
of April 1825

Witness   Margaret Horniblow   {Seal}

Jno M Jones

Henry Flury Junr

Codicil; It is my will & desire that
the foregoing devise be so far altered, that
my negro girl Harriet be given to my niece
Mary Matilda Norcom Daughter of Dr James Norcom;
and I further give & bequeath to my said niece
my Bureau & work table & their contents—

The above Codicil was
acknowledgd before us the 3 day of July
the year above write

Henry Flury

Jno Norcom.

With this will,
Margaret Horniblow,
Harriet Jacobs's
first mistress, gave
away "my negro
girl Harriet" and
"my bureau &
work table & their
contents" to her
young niece.

daughter, a child of five years old. So vanished our hopes. My mistress had taught me the *precepts* of God's Word: "Thou shalt love thy neighbor as thyself." "Whatsoever ye would that men should do unto you, do ye even so unto them." But I was her slave, and I suppose she did not recognize me as her neighbor.

rules

Mary Prince

Looking back on her life, Mary Prince said that as a child she did not "understand rightly" her condition as a slave. Born into slavery on the island of Bermuda, Mary lived happily at first with her mother and brothers and sisters. They were all the property of a young girl of Mary's age, Betsey Williams, and they considered Betsey's mother, Mrs. Williams, to be their mistress.

When Mary was twelve, Mrs. Williams died and Mary learned that Mr. Williams planned to remarry, and to pay for his wedding by selling her and her sisters, Hannah and Dinah. Although they belonged to Williams's daughter, Betsey, there was nothing the young Betsey could do to prevent their sale. When the day of parting arrived, Mary's mother had to take her three daughters to the slave market to be sold. There Mary learned what it meant to be someone else's property.

AT length the *vendue* master, who was to offer us for sale like sheep or cattle, arrived, and asked my mother which was the eldest. She said nothing, but pointed to me. He took me by the hand, and led me out into the middle of the street, and, turning me slowly round, exposed me to the view of those who attended the vendue. I was soon surrounded by strange men, who examined and handled me in the same manner that a butcher would a calf or a lamb he was about to purchase, and

auction

who talked about my shape and size in like words—as if I could no more understand their meaning than the dumb beasts. I was then put up to sale. The bidding commenced at a few *pounds,* and gradually rose to fifty-seven, when I was *knocked down* to the highest bidder; and the people who stood by said that I had fetched a great sum for so young a slave.

Bermuda money sold

I then saw my sisters led forth, and sold to different owners; so that we had not the sad satisfaction of being partners in bondage. When the sale was over, my mother hugged and kissed us, and mourned over us, begging of us to keep up a good heart, and do our duty to our new masters. It was a sad parting; one went one way, one another, and our poor mammy went home with nothing.

THE ENSLAVED FAMILY

The enslaved family was never safe. Enslaved people belonged to their owners, not to their own families. They were property, to be bought and sold, traded or given away.

GROWING NATION, BROKEN FAMILIES

After the American Revolution, the new nation expanded westward and more and more enslaved families were broken apart. Slaveholders raised and sold slaves to slave traders, who took them to the slave markets in New Orleans. There, they were sold for work on the new frontier plantations. Some slaveholders refused to break up families through sale. But even when their consciences forbid them to do so, the laws of slavery allowed it.

Enslaved men and women were not allowed to marry legally. Enslaved mothers and fathers had no legal rights as parents. In most places, enslaved people were forbidden to have family surnames.

Despite the fact that they could be split up, slaves managed to teach their children about their families and their roots. This Henry Ossawa Tanner painting shows banjo skill being passed from one generation to the next.

They were forced to take the last names of their owners. In some places, enslaved siblings could not even call each other "brother" or "sister." They were punished for acknowledging their kin.

Still, most slaveholders wanted their slaves to form families. Families meant children, and children could be sold, which meant wealth. Slaveholders also thought that slaves who lived in families were easier to control, because they were afraid of being separated from the people they loved.

Enslaved men and women knew their families might be broken up. Still, they worked hard to take care of their family members, to raise their children, and to teach them about their kin. Unable to read or write, they could not keep family records, but they told and retold family stories. They kept family surnames, often in secret. They gave their children the name of a grandmother or grandfather, a favorite aunt or uncle. In this way, they remembered their ancestors and the people who had died, been left behind, or sold away.

"Old Elizabeth"

Separated from those they loved, many enslaved people found comfort in their religion. One such person, known only as Elizabeth, was born into slavery in Maryland in 1766. Her parents were both religious people, and Elizabeth herself began to feel a spiritual presence in her life when she was only five. This presence became very important to her after she was parted from her family. Alone in a new place, Elizabeth comforted herself with prayer.

Elizabeth gained her freedom at the age of thirty, and went on to become a preacher. Many years later, when she was ninety-seven years old, she told the story of her young life in the book, *Memoir of Old Elizabeth, A Coloured Woman.*

This painting by English artist Eyre Crowe shows a slave market in Virginia. As buyers talk in the doorway, slaves wait to learn their fate and the fate of their families.

In the eleventh year of my age, my master sent me to another farm, several miles from my parents, brothers, and sisters, which was a great trouble to me. At last I grew so lonely and sad I thought I should die, if I did not see my mother. I asked the *overseer* if I might go, but being positively denied, I concluded to go without his knowledge. When I reached home my

manager

mother was away. I set off and walked twenty miles before I found her. I *staid* with her for several days, and we returned together. Next day I was sent back to my new place, which renewed my sorrow. At parting, my mother told me that I had "nobody in the wide world to look to but God." These words fell upon my heart with *pondrous* weight, and seemed to add to my grief. I went back repeating as I went, "none but God in the wide world." On reaching the farm, I found the overseer was displeased at me for going without his *liberty.* He tied me with a rope, and gave me some *stripes* of which I carried the marks for weeks.

stayed

heavy

permission
lashings

After this time, finding as my mother said, I had none in the world to look to but God, I *betook myself to prayer,* and in every lonely place I found an altar. I mourned sore like a dove and chattered forth my sorrow, moaning in the corners of the field, and under the fences.

prayed

I continued in this state for about six months, feeling as though my head were waters, and I could do nothing but weep. I lost my appetite, and not being able to take enough food to sustain nature, I became so weak I had but little strength to work; still I was required to do all my duty. One evening, after the duties of the day were ended, I thought I could not live over the night, so threw myself on a bench, expecting to die, and without being prepared to meet my Maker; and my spirit cried within me, must I die in this state, and be banished from Thy presence forever? I *own* I am a sinner in Thy sight, and not fit to live where thou art. Still it was my *fervent* desire that the Lord would pardon me. Just at this season, I saw with my spiritual eye, an awful gulf of misery. As I thought I was about to plunge into it, I heard a voice saying, "rise up and pray," which strengthened me. I fell on my knees and prayed the best I could the Lord's prayer.

admit
burning

The Reverend James W. C. Pennington

Not all enslaved families were broken apart. James W. C. Pennington came from a large family that had remained together on the Eastern Shore of the Chesapeake Bay, in Maryland.

The Penningtons suffered as a family, even though they were not separated. James's parents were constantly reminded that their master—and not they—had authority over the family. Like many slave parents, the Penningtons also endured the humiliation of being punished in front of their own children.

In 1828, after watching his father being beaten, James Pennington decided to escape to the North. Trained as a blacksmith in slavery, in the North he became a famous writer and preacher. In his autobiography, *The Fugitive Blacksmith,* he remembered the day that changed his life.

M y father, among other numerous and responsible duties, *discharged* that of shepherd to a large and valuable flock *performed* of Merino sheep. This morning he was engaged in the tenderest of a shepherd's duties: a little lamb, not able to go alone, lost its mother; he was feeding it by hand. He had been keeping it in the house for several days. As he stooped over it in the yard, with a *vessel* of new milk he had obtained, with which to feed *bottle* it, my master came along, and without the least *provocation,* be- *cause* gan by asking,

"Bazil, have you fed the flock?"

"Yes, sir."

"Were you away yesterday?"

"No, sir."

"Do you know why these boys [other workers] have not got home this morning yet?"

"No, sir, I have not seen any of them since Saturday night."

"By *the Eternal,* I'll make them know their *hour.* The fact is, I have too many of you; my people are getting to be the most careless, lazy, and worthless in the country."

God; work time

"Master," said my father, "I am always at my post; Monday morning never finds me off the plantation."

"Hush Bazil! I shall have to sell some of you; and then the rest will have enough to do; I have not work enough to keep you all tightly employed; I have too many of you."

All this was said in an angry, threatening, and exceedingly insulting tone. My father was a high-spirited man, and feeling deeply the insult, replied to the last expression, "If I am one too many, sir, give me a chance to get a purchaser, and I am willing to be sold when it may suit you."

"Bazil, I told you to hush!" and suiting the action to the word, he drew forth the *cowhide* from under his arm, fell upon him with most savage cruelty, and inflicted fifteen or twenty severe *stripes* with all his strength, over [my father's] shoulders and the small of his back. As he raised himself upon his toes, and gave the last stripe, he said, "By the * * * I will make you know that I am master of your tongue as well as of your time!"

whip

lashings

Let me ask any *one of Anglo-Saxon blood and spirit,* how would you expect a [son] to feel at such a sight?

white person

This act created *an open rupture* with our family—each member felt the deep insult that had been inflicted upon our head; the spirit of the whole family was roused; we talked of it in our nightly gatherings, and showed it in our daily *melancholy aspect.* The *oppressor* saw this, and with the heartlessness that was in perfect keeping with the first insult, commenced a series of tauntings, threatenings, and insinuations, with a view to crush the spirit of the whole family.

a breaking point

long faces
cruel master

Although it was some time after this event before I took the decisive step, yet in my mind and spirit, I never was a [Slave] after it.

Abream Scriven

Together or apart, the enslaved family suffered. As long as it lasted, slavery brought misery to people who deeply loved one another. In 1858, only a few years before slavery ended, Abream Scriven of Georgia was sold by his owner to a New Orleans slave trader. Unlike most enslaved people, Abream could read and write, and from the slave trader's yard in Savannah, he wrote a good-bye letter to his wife Dinah.

Savannah Sept the 19 1858

Dinah Jones

    My Dear wife I take the pleasure of writing you these few [lines] with much regret to inform you that I am Sold to a man by the name of Peterson *atreader* . . . in new orleans. I am here   *a slave trader*
yet But I expect to go before long but when I get there I will write and let you know where I am. My Dear I want to Send you Some things but I do not know who to Send them By but I will *thry* to get them to you and my children. Give my love to   *try*
my father & mother and tell them good Bye for me. and if we Shall not meet in this world I hope to meet in heaven. My Dear wife for you and my Children my pen cannot Express the *griffe*   *grief*
I feel to be parted from you all

I remain your *truly* husband until Death   *true*
Abream Scriven

THE WORK OF SLAVERY

Slavery was a kind of legal robbery. Slaveholders, instead of paying their workers, simply stole their labor. It was cheaper to buy and work slaves than to pay free workers. Settlers in the New World increased their wealth and property by making property of others.

IN THE NORTH

The work done by enslaved people changed over time, and from place to place. In the North, the early Puritans lived in small communities that tightly controlled the religious and social conduct of their members. Settlers in such communities rarely held African slaves. They preferred to use indentured English servants, whose customs and religion they shared. Many Puritans also disliked slavery for moral and religious reasons.

Outside of such communities, however, Northerners used enslaved labor. Enslaved men and women worked on small farms in western Connecticut and Massachusetts, and on the estates of large landowners in New York and Rhode Island. They helped to build the new cities and roads. They worked in the growing industries of New England—shipbuilding, lumbering, mining, tanning, whaling, and fishing. Slaves also created wealth for New England shipowners, whose ships took part in the Atlantic slave trade.

IN THE SOUTH

In the southern colonies, slavery developed differently. Unlike the Puritans, southern colonists did not live in strict, religious communities. They had greater social freedom, but their greater freedom meant a greater lack of freedom for their slaves. Southern settlers used enslaved labor for everything they wanted done. For this reason, slavery took root more deeply in the South than it did in the North. By the time of the American Revolution, the southern economy had become completely dependent upon slave labor.

In the 1600s and early 1700s, southern settlers used slave labor to clear the land and establish farms and to raise the early cash crops of tobacco and rice. Like Northerners, they also used slave labor to build cities, roads, and bridges, to dig canals, and to mine the land. As the world market for southern tobacco, rice, sugar, and cotton grew larger, Southerners imported more and more Africans to work the land. And they pushed westward, using slave labor to clear and farm new land, and to build new settlements and cities.

Throughout the South, enslaved men and women labored on both small farms and large plantations. In both cases, the work was unending and backbreaking. But on the larger plantations, the work was also more varied. Large planters needed many different workers to keep their plantations going—carpenters, blacksmiths, gardeners, cooks, horse trainers, personal servants, seamstresses, and more. For this reason, people enslaved on large plantations had a much better chance of becoming skilled workers than those on small farms.

Solomon Northup

Solomon Northup was born and raised a free man in upstate New York. He became a carpenter and a farmer, married a free woman named Anne Hampton, and had three children. But like many free

Although slaves worked at many different jobs in both the North and South, they were essential to the South's main industry: cotton. So important was cotton to the South's economy that it was called "King Cotton." This painting shows slaves participating in every aspect of "King Cotton": picking it, gathering it, loading it, and transporting it—all without being paid.

African Americans, Solomon Northup was kidnapped and sold into slavery. This happened in 1841, when he was thirty-two years old.

For the next twelve years, until his rescue, Northup slaved on frontier plantations in the Red River region of Louisiana. He spent his last eight years of slavery on Edwin Epps's small plantation on the Bayou Boeuf, planting, raising, and picking cotton. Solomon Northup was a careful observer of all that went on around him. In his autobiography, *Twelve Years A Slave,* published in 1853, he gave an exact picture of the cotton-picking season.

In the latter part of August begins the cotton picking season. At this time each slave is presented with a sack. A strap is fastened to it, which goes over the neck, holding the mouth of the sack breast high, while the bottom reaches nearly to the ground. Each one is also presented with a large basket that will hold about two barrels. This is to put the cotton in when the sack is filled. The baskets are carried to the field and placed at the beginning of the rows.

When a new hand, one unaccustomed to the business, is sent for the first time into the field, he is *whipped up smartly,* and *whipped hard* made for that day to pick as fast as he can possibly. At night it [his cotton] is weighed, so that his capability in cotton picking is known. He must bring in the same weight each night following. If it falls short, it is considered evidence that he has been *laggard,* and a greater or less number of lashes is the penalty. *slow*

An ordinary day's work is considered two hundred pounds. A slave who is accustomed to picking, is punished, if he or she brings in a less quantity than that. There is a great difference among them [slaves] as regards this kind of labor. Some of them seem to have a natural knack, or quickness, which enables them to pick with great *celerity,* and with both hands, while others, *speed* with whatever practice or *industry,* are utterly unable to come *hard work* up to the ordinary standard. Such hands are taken from the cotton field and employed in other business. Patsey, of whom I shall have more to say, was known as the most remarkable cotton picker on Bayou Boeuf. She picked with both hands and with such surprising rapidity, that five hundred pounds a day was not unusual for her.

Each one is *tasked,* therefore, according to his picking abilities, none, however, to come short of two hundred weight. I, being unskillful always in that business, would have satisfied my master by bringing in the latter quantity, while on the other hand, Patsey would surely have been beaten if she failed to produce twice as much.

given work

The cotton grows from five to seven feet high, each stalk having a great many branches, shooting out in all directions, and *lapping* each other above the water furrow.

overlapping

There are few sights more pleasant to the eye, than a wide cotton field when it is in the bloom. It presents an appearance of purity, like an immaculate expanse of light, new-fallen snow.

Sometimes the slave picks down one side of a row, and back upon the other, but more usually, there is one on either side, gathering all that has blossomed, leaving the unopened *bolls* for a succeeding picking. When the sack is filled, it is emptied into the basket and *trodden* down. It is necessary to be extremely careful the first time going through the field, in order not to break the branches off the stalks. The cotton will not bloom upon a broken branch. Epps never failed to inflict the severest *chastisement* on the unlucky servant who, either carelessly or unavoidably, was guilty in the least degree in this respect.

bunches of cotton

stamped

punishment

The hands are required to be in the cotton fields as soon as it is light in the morning, and, with the exception of ten or fifteen minutes, which is given them at noon to swallow their allowance of cold bacon, they are not permitted to be a moment idle until it is too dark to see, and when the moon is full, they often times labor till the middle of the night. They do not dare to stop even at dinner time, nor return to the quarters, however, late it be, until the order to halt is given by the driver.

Frederick Douglass

Frederick Douglass spent twenty-three years in slavery before escaping to the North. He was born and raised on a large plantation in rural Maryland. When Douglass was eight or nine years old, he was sent to Baltimore to live with Hugh and Sophia Auld, his owner's brother and sister-in-law. There he had to do light household work and take care of the Aulds' son.

Like many enslaved men and women, Douglass preferred working in a city to working on a farm or plantation. In the city there was more freedom. Slaves might hire out their time, working a job and giving their masters some or most of their wages. In this way, people enslaved in cities might save a little money of their own and also become skilled workers.

When Frederick Douglass went to work building boats at Gardner's Shipyard in 1836, he hoped to do both. But earning money for his master proved easier than learning a skill for himself.

I was put there to learn how to *calk.* It, however, proved a very unfavorable place for the accomplishment of this object. Mr. Gardner was engaged that spring in building two large *man-of-war brigs,* professedly for the Mexican government. The vessels were to be launched in the July of that year, and in failure thereof, Mr. Gardner was to lose a considerable sum; so that when I entered, all was hurry. There was no time to learn any thing. Every man had to do that which he knew how to do. In entering the shipyard, my orders from Mr. Gardner were, to do

waterproof

battleships

Slaves, some only young children, labor in a tobacco
factory in Lynchburg, Virginia.

whatever the carpenters commanded me to do. This was placing
me at the beck and call of about seventy-five men. I was to
regard all these as masters. Their word was to be my law. My
situation was a most *trying* one. At times I needed a dozen pair
of hands. I was called a dozen ways in the space of a single
minute. Three or four voices would strike my ear at the same
moment. It was—"Fred., come help me to *cant* this timber
here."—"Fred., come carry this timber yonder."—"Fred., bring

frustrating

set at an angle

that roller here."—"Fred., go get a fresh can of water."—"Fred., come help me saw off the end of this timber."—"Fred., go quick, and get the crowbar."—"Fred., hold on the end of this *fall*."— *rope* "Fred., go to the blacksmith's shop, and get a new punch."— "Hurra, Fred.! run and bring me a cold chisel."—"I say, Fred., *bear* a hand, and get up a fire as quick as lightning under that *give* *steambox*."—"Halloo, nigger! come, turn this grindstone."— *boiler* "Come, come! move, move! and *bowse* this timber forward."— *pull* "I say, darky, blast your eyes, why don't you heat up some *pitch?*"—"Halloo! halloo! halloo!" (Three voices at the same time.) *tar* "Come here!—Go there!—Hold on where you are! Damn you, if you move, I'll knock your brains out!"

This was my school for eight months.

Mary Prince

Like Solomon Northup and Frederick Douglass, Mary Prince slaved hard. Sold from one West Indian island to another, Mary had no time to herself and never learned to read or write. When her last owners brought her to England in 1828, she claimed her freedom. By that time, slavery was illegal in England, and any enslaved person who set foot on English soil became free.

Mary Prince told the story of her enslavement to the English abolitionists who helped her escape. They wrote it down in *The History of Mary Prince, A West Indian Slave*. There, Mary told of working to extract salt from the ponds on Turks Island, where she had been taken at the age of seventeen.

My new master was one of the owners or holders of the salt ponds, and he received a certain sum for every slave that worked upon his premises, whether they were young or old. This sum was allowed him out of the profits arising from the salt works. I was immediately sent to work in the salt water with the rest of the slaves. This work was perfectly new to me. I was given a half barrel and a shovel, and had to stand up to my knees in the water, from four o'clock in the morning till nine, when we were given some Indian corn boiled in water, which we were obliged to swallow as fast as we could for fear the rain should come on and melt the salt. We were then called again to our tasks, and worked through the heat of the day; the sun flaming upon our heads like fire, and raising salt blisters in those parts which were not completely covered. Our feet and legs, from standing in the salt water for so many hours, soon became full of dreadful boils, which eat down in some cases to the very bone, afflicting the sufferers with great torment. We came home at twelve; ate our corn soup, called [blawly], as fast as we could, and went back to our employment till dark at night. We then shovelled up the salt in large heaps, and went down to the sea, where we washed the *pickle* from our limbs, and *brine* cleaned the *barrows* and shovels from the salt. When we re- *wheelbarrows* turned to the house, our master gave us each our allowance of raw Indian corn, which we pounded in a mortar and boiled in water for our suppers.

We slept in a long shed, divided into narrow *slips,* like the *compartments* stalls used for cattle. Boards fixed upon stakes driven into the ground, without mat or covering, were our only beds. On Sun- days, after we had washed the salt bags, and done other work required of us, we went into the bush and cut the long soft grass, of which we made *trusses* for our legs and feet to rest *supports* upon, for they were so full of the salt boils that we could get no rest lying upon the bare boards.

RESISTANCE

Wherever enslaved people worked, whatever work they did, their work belonged to others, not to themselves. For this reason, most enslaved people worked unwillingly. Some were able to escape, and we shall see how they did in a later chapter. But those who could not escape slavery, or who chose to stay put, resisted it in many ways, large and small.

ARMED REBELLIONS

Many times during the long years of slavery, enslaved people took up arms together to rebel against the system that entrapped them. The best known of these rebellions occurred in Stono, South Carolina, in 1739; in Richmond, Virginia, in 1800; in Charleston, South Carolina, in 1822; and in Southhampton County, Virginia, in 1831, and their leaders are remembered today as men who gave their lives to help end slavery. Their names are Cato, Gabriel Prosser, Denmark Vesey, and Nat Turner.

The most famous armed resistance to slavery in the United States was led by Nat Turner on August 22, 1831. Turner and his followers killed about sixty white people in Virginia. More than one hundred blacks were killed in revenge. This engraving shows Turner's capture on October 20. Two weeks later he was hanged.

The rebellions these men led were defeated by the slaveholding community. In this sense, they failed in their immediate goals. But Cato, Gabriel Prosser, Denmark Vesey, and Nat Turner each struck a vigorous blow against slavery. The heroic actions of these men, and the men and women who joined them, sent a clear message to the nation: Enslaved people were willing to fight and die for their freedom. In the ongoing war against slavery, it was a message that gave courage to many others.

DAY-TO-DAY RESISTANCE

Armed resistance to slavery was rare, but day-to-day resistance was not. Always and everywhere, enslaved men, women, and children resisted the slaveholders who worked them.

For most enslaved people, the workday lasted from before sunrise to well after dark—"from can see to can't," as they put it. Overworked and tired, enslaved men and women had many ways of stopping work or lightening their work load. They ran away for a time to rest, even though they knew they would be punished when they returned. They broke their tools and other equipment. They burned crops and farm buildings. They pretended to be sick.

Enslaved people were often cruelly abused. Slaveholders beat their slaves to make them work harder, to teach them their "place," to set an example for other slaves, or simply because they were drunk or angry and the law was on their side. To avoid beatings, enslaved men and women often ran away for a time. Or they stayed where they were and fought back. Some even killed masters who were especially cruel, although to do so meant certain death. In these ways and many others, those held in slavery fought to make their daily lives more bearable.

Fannie

Fannie was enslaved on a small farm in Eden, Tennessee, during the final years of slavery. She was a strong, quick worker who could do anything. She worked as a field hand. She cooked, washed, ironed, spun cloth, and nursed the sick. Fannie also had a temper, and she would never allow anyone to beat her. No one could make her do anything she didn't want to do. Fannie's daughter, Cornelia, remembered her mother as "the smartest black woman in Eden."

Fannie did not live to see the end of slavery, but her daughter Cornelia lived well into the twentieth century. She never forgot the woman who had raised her, and in 1930, when she was ninety-six years old, Cornelia told Fannie's story.

One day my mother's temper ran wild. For some reason Mistress Jennings struck her with a stick. Ma struck back and a fight followed. Mr. Jennings was not at home and the children became frightened and ran upstairs. For half an hour they wrestled in the kitchen. Mistress, seeing that she could not get the better of ma, ran out in the road, with ma right on her heels. In the road, my mother flew into her again. The thought seemed to race across my mother's mind to tear mistress' clothing off her body. She suddenly began to tear Mistress Jennings' clothes off. She caught hold, pulled, ripped and tore. Poor mistress was nearly naked when the storekeeper got to them and pulled ma off.

"Why, Fannie, what do you mean by that?" he asked.

"Why, I'll kill her, I'll kill her dead if she ever strikes me again."

I have never been able to find out the why of the whole thing. My mother was in a rage for two days, and when pa asked her about it and told her that she shouldn't have done it, it was all that Aunt Caroline could do to keep her from giving him the same dose of medicine.

"No explaining necessary. You are chicken-livered, and you couldn't understand." This was all ma would say about it.

Pa heard Mr. Jennings say that Fannie would have to be whipped by law. He told ma. Two mornings afterwards, two men came in at the big gate, one with a long lash in his hand. I was in the yard and I hoped they couldn't find ma. To my surprise, I saw her running around the house, straight in the direction of the men. She must have seen them coming. I should have known that she wouldn't hide. She knew what they were coming for, and she intended to meet them halfway. She swooped upon them like a hawk on chickens. I believe they were afraid of her or thought she was crazy. One man had a long beard which she grabbed with one hand, and the lash with the other. Her body was made strong with madness. She was a good match for them. Mr. Jennings came and pulled her away. I don't know what would have happened if he hadn't come at that moment, for one man had already pulled his gun out. Ma did not see the gun until Mr. Jennings came up. On catching sight of it, she said, "Use your gun, use it and blow my brains out if you will."

Master sent her to the cabin and he talked with the man for a long time. I had watched the whole scene with hands calmly clasped in front of me. I felt no urge to do anything but look on.

That evening Mistress Jennings came down to the cabin. She stopped at the door and called my mother. Ma came out.

"Well, Fannie," she said, "I'll have to send you away. You won't be whipped, and I'm afraid you'll get killed. They have to knock you down like a beef."

"I'll go to hell or anywhere else, but I won't be whipped," ma answered.

"You can't take the baby, Fannie, Aunt Mary can keep it with the other children."

Mother said nothing at this. That night, ma and pa sat up late, talking over things, I guess. Pa loved ma and I heard him say, "I'm going, too, Fannie." About a week later, she called me and told me that she and pa were going to leave me the next day, that they were going to Memphis. She didn't know for how long.

"But don't be abused, Puss." She always called me Puss. My right name was Cornelia. I cannot tell in words the feelings I had at that time. My sorrow knew no bound. My very soul seemed to cry out, "Gone, gone, gone forever." I cried until my eyes looked like balls of fire. I felt for the first time in my life that I had been abused. How cruel it was to take my mother and father from me, I thought. My mother had been right. Slavery was cruel, so very cruel.

Thus my mother and father were hired to Tennessee. The next morning they were to leave. I saw ma working around with the baby under her arms as if it had been a bundle of some kind. Pa came up to the cabin with an old mare for ma to ride, and an old mule for himself. Mr. Jennings was with him.

"Fannie, leave the baby with Aunt Mary," said Mr. Jennings very quietly.

At this, ma took the baby by its feet, a foot in each hand, and with the baby's head swinging downward, she vowed to smash its brains out before she'd leave it. Tears were streaming down her face. It was seldom that ma cried, and everyone knew that she meant every word. Ma took her baby with her. . . .

I decided to follow my mother's example. I intended to fight, and if I couldn't fight I'd kick; and if I couldn't kick, I'd bite. The children from the big house played with my brothers, but I got out of the bunch. I stopped playing with them. I didn't care about them, so why play with them? At different times I got into scraps with them. Everyone began to say, "Cornelia is the spit of her mother. She is going to be just like Fannie." And I delighted in hearing this. I wanted to be like ma now.

Like Fannie, the woman in this painting, Margaret Garner, was willing to kill her children rather than lose them to slavery. Garner escaped slavery in 1856 but was captured and returned to her master. She killed one child and wounded another. When her remaining children were taken away, she killed herself.

Solomon Northup

During his twelve years of enslavement in Louisiana, Solomon Northup had three different owners. He remembered the first, William Ford, as a good man. But when Ford needed money to pay his debts, he sold Northup to John Tibeats. Tibeats was a violent man who hated Northup and constantly found fault with his work. More than once he tried to beat Northup, but Northup always resisted. More and more enraged, Tibeats finally picked a fight and came after Northup with a hatchet.

It was a moment of life or death. The sharp, bright blade of the hatchet glittered in the sun. In another instant it would be buried in my brain, and yet in that instant—so quick will a man's thoughts come to him in such a fearful *strait*—I reasoned with myself. If I stood still, my doom was certain; if I fled, ten chances to one the hatchet, flying from his hand with a too-deadly and *unerring* aim, would strike me in the back. There was but one course to take. Springing towards him with all my power, and meeting him full half-way, before he could bring down the blow, with one hand I caught his uplifted arm, with the other seized him by the throat. We stood looking each other in the eyes. In his I could see murder. I felt as if I had a serpent by the neck, watching [for] the slightest relaxation of my grip, to coil itself round my body, crushing and stinging it to death. I thought to scream aloud, trusting that some ear might catch the sound—but [the overseer] was away; the hands were in the field; there was no living soul in sight or hearing.

situation

accurate

The good *genius,* which thus far through life has saved me from the hands of violence, at that moment suggested a lucky thought. With a vigorous and sudden kick, that brought him on one knee, with a groan, I released my hold upon his throat, snatched the hatchet, and cast it beyond reach.

spirit

That didn't stop Tibeats. He grabbed a club, and when Northup took that away from him, Tibeats tried to pick up an axe that was stuck under a board. Northup wrestled Tibeats for the axe, and later recalled what went through his mind during the struggle.

Life is dear to every living thing; the worm that crawls upon the ground will struggle for it. At that moment it was dear to me, enslaved and treated as I was.

Not able to unloose his hand, once more I seized him by the throat, and this time, with a vice-like grip that soon relaxed his hold. He became *pliant* and *unstrung.* His face, that had been white with passion, was now black from suffocation. Those small serpent eyes that spat such venom, were now full of horror— two great white orbs *starting* from their sockets!

There was a ''lurking devil'' in my heart that prompted me to kill the human blood-hound on the spot—to retain the grip on his accursed throat till the breath of life was gone! I dared not murder him, and I dared not let him live. If I killed him, my life must pay the *forfeit*—if he lived, my life only would satisfy his vengeance. A voice within whispered [to] me to *fly.*

weak; confused

bulging

penalty
escape

LITERACY

We don't usually think of reading and writing as acts of resistance. But they were supreme acts of resistance for enslaved people, who had to fight for their learning just as they had to fight for food. Not only did they lack books, teachers, and schools—the law also made it a crime to teach reading and writing to slaves.

THE ANTI-LITERACY LAWS

In the beginning of North American slavery, most slaveholders simply refused to teach their slaves how to read and write, or to give them schools or teachers. They wanted from their slaves only the work of their bodies, not of their minds. When enslaved people learned anyway, some colonies passed laws against teaching slaves to read and write. These were called "anti-literacy laws." South Carolina passed the first such anti-literacy law in 1740. It stated that literate slaves were "great inconveniences," and it fined teachers 100 pounds for every slave they taught to read and write.

HOW ILLITERACY KEPT PEOPLE ENSLAVED

Slaveholders used the illiteracy of enslaved people to control their movements. Enslaved persons traveling away from their owners had to carry written passes, or "permissions," stating the name of their owners and the nature of their errands. They could be stopped at any time, by any white person, and asked for their passes. This in turn made escape more difficult. Unable to write their own passes, escaping slaves had to avoid anyone who might ask them for a pass.

Illiteracy worked against enslaved people in other ways as well. For example, when a slaveholder wanted a slave beaten, but didn't want to do it himself, he might send that person to the local jail with a note asking the jailer to perform the beating. Unable to read the note, the slave would walk into the trap.

Slaveholders knew that without the ability to read and write enslaved people could not write to each other. They could not plan rebellion together in writing. They could not read and study maps of the areas where they were held, or discover in books new ways of escaping or new places to escape to. Enslaved people could not read in books about their own right to freedom. They could not even read the laws that held them in slavery.

LITERACY AND FREEDOM

Slaveholders knew that literacy went hand in hand with freedom. Enslaved people knew it too, and they struggled, often in secret, to learn to read and write. They learned from each other, from the free

African Americans around them, and from white Americans who felt that everybody should be literate.

The people, black and white, who taught slaves to read and write broke the law, and often they were fined or jailed for their teaching. The enslaved people who learned were also punished. But their new skills could not be taken from them.

Frederick Douglass

No one valued literacy more than the great Frederick Douglass. For Douglass, literacy and freedom were almost the same thing.

When Douglass moved to Baltimore, his new mistress, Sophia Auld, began teaching him to read, but when Hugh Auld found out what his wife was doing, he put an end to it. The lessons stopped, but the young Frederick learned something he never forgot. He wrote of it in his first autobiography, *The Narrative of the Life of Frederick Douglass, An American Slave, Written by Himself.*

M r. Auld found out what was going on, and at once forbade Mrs. Auld to instruct me further, telling her, among other things, that it was unlawful, as well as unsafe, to teach a slave to read. To use his own words, further, he said, "If you give a nigger an inch, he will take an *ell*. A nigger should know nothing but to obey his master—to do as he is told to do. Learning would [spoil] the best nigger in the world. Now," said he, "if you teach that nigger (speaking of myself) how to read, there would be no keeping him. It would forever unfit him to be a slave. He would at once become unmanageable, and of no value to his master. As to himself, it could do him no good, but a great deal of harm. It would make him discontented and unhappy." These words sank deep into my heart, stirred up sentiments within that lay slumbering, and called into existence an

yard

Frederick Douglass. Perhaps more than any other writing by a slave, his book *Narrative of the Life of Frederick Douglass, An American Slave, Written by Himself* helped open people's eyes to the evils of slavery in the United States and bring about its end. For Douglass, reading and writing were nothing less than the keys to freedom.

entirely new train of thought. It was a new and special *revelation*, explaining dark and mysterious things, with which my youthful understanding had struggled, but struggled in vain. I now understood what had been to me a most *perplexing difficulty—to wit*, the white man's power to enslave the black man. It was a grand achievement, and I prized it highly. From that moment, I understood the pathway from slavery to freedom.

discovery

*puzzling
question—namely*

ESCAPING SLAVERY

For more than two hundred years, people were held in slavery in the United States. During that time, thousands of men, women, and children managed to escape. They did so in different ways at different times. As the nation and its borders changed, so did the escape from slavery.

Some people were freed by their owners, or "manumitted." But as slavery grew older, new slave laws made manumission harder and harder. Some people were able to buy their freedom, but this too become harder as the years went by. A few people sued and won their freedom in court. But most enslaved people who managed to escape did so by running away.

EARLY ESCAPE ROUTES: 1641–1819

Before the American Revolution, the English settlements were surrounded by Indian land. Enslaved Indians often escaped from the settlements to return to their people. Enslaved Africans did the same,

In escaping slavery, men and women risked attack by slave hunters, hostile whites, and even animals. This painting shows runaway slaves defending themselves against dogs trained to catch slaves.

sometimes becoming members of Indian communities. But as the Indian people were pushed farther and farther west, escape of this kind became impossible.

Before the Louisiana Purchase from France in 1803, people enslaved along the western frontier escaped to freedom by crossing over into French territory. Before 1819, people enslaved in South Carolina and Georgia escaped south to Spanish Florida. But when the United States purchased these lands and expanded its territory, slavery also expanded, and the western and southern escape routes were cut off. After 1819, the best way out of slavery lay to the North.

ESCAPE TO THE NORTH

In the years after the American Revolution, the northern states one by one outlawed slavery. By 1818, when Illinois became a state, a line stretching from the Atlantic Ocean to the Mississippi River divided the "free soil" of the North from the slave states of the South. Slaves to the south of this line now escaped north across it.

The Ohio River ran along this line for approximately 1,000 miles, dividing the free North from the slave South. Slaves in Kentucky and parts of Tennessee and Virginia escaped across the river into Illinois, Indiana, and Ohio. People farther east, in Maryland and eastern Virginia, went north to Philadelphia or New York City.

Escape from the deep South to the North was harder, but some people managed it. They stowed away on boats going north along the coast or up the Mississippi River. They posed as free men and women and took a boat or train north. William and Ellen Craft, an enslaved husband and wife, made a daring escape north out of Georgia. With Ellen dressed as a man, they rode the train north, a thousand miles to Philadelphia, posing as master and slave.

THE UNDERGROUND RAILROAD

Escaping or "fugitive" slaves had many enemies, north and south. Slave catchers were everywhere. Some people turned in fugitive slaves to collect reward money. Others turned them in for nothing.

But fugitive slaves also had many friends, north and south, black and white. The "Underground Railroad" was a group of such people. Its members worked to help escaping slaves reach freedom. From one secret hiding place to another, the Underground Railroad sped fugitives north to the free states, and beyond to Canada.

One of the Underground Railroad's most famous "conductors"

was Harriet Tubman. Born into slavery in Maryland, she escaped in 1848, leaving her husband, parents, and siblings behind. Nineteen times Harriet Tubman went back across the line into the slave South, bringing out not only her family but hundreds of other slaves. At one time there was a reward of $40,000 for her capture. But Harriet Tubman was never caught.

THE FUGITIVE SLAVE LAW OF 1850

To stop the flow of fugitive slaves north, the South forced the passage of a new law in 1850. Called "The Fugitive Slave Law," it, in effect, did away with free soil. Now, Americans everywhere were made to turn over fugitive slaves. To help slaves escape became a crime. Federal marshals could search any house where they thought a fugitive might be hiding. Fugitives who were caught had no right to a jury trial. They were brought before judges, who decided their cases. The new law stated that judges who returned fugitives to the South would get ten dollars, while those who set them free would get only five.

As a result of the Fugitive Slave Law, people who had been living freely in the North for many years were captured and taken back into slavery. Many went into hiding. Others left for England or Canada, where the law could not touch them. People everywhere who hated slavery called for resistance to the new law. Some called for a new revolution, to end slavery once and for all.

Ten years later, in 1861, the Civil War broke out.

Andrew Jackson

Born into slavery in Kentucky in 1814, Andrew Jackson made his escape at the age of twenty-five. Like so many others, he made the "long walk" north, traveling by night to avoid other people. But on his fourth day out, Andrew chose to travel in daylight and was almost caught.

When he told the story of his life a few years later in the *Narrative of Andrew Jackson,* he remembered fighting off the men who tried to take him back into slavery.

Just upon the point of scaling a fence, a man sprang up like a tiger from the side of a log and struck at me. Quick as I could, I turned and ran a few steps and bounded over the fence. Just as my feet struck the ground, a club grazed my shoulder, but did me no harm; a little way ahead, I saw another man and dog, with a boy and horse. The man had a gun. Now, thought I, are my hopes blasted. I had heard about the Israelites when they fled from the slavery of Egypt. I thought I was like them. Before and behind me are death. I almost sank down with despair—but rallied again, determined to *sell* my life and liberty *give up* together, or to gain them. And with that strength, which even surprised me, I ran for the bushes—the dog pursuing me in the lead, followed by the two men and boy—the man being on horseback. As the dog came up, I seized a stone and fortunately hit him in the head, leaving him stiff upon the ground. The man on the horse soon came up and uttering *oaths* which made my *curses* blood chill, almost, commanded me to stop. I did so—but only to draw back my trusty *hickory,* and by a well directed blow sent *stick* him reeling from his unsaddled horse. He soon recovered, however, as the blow only stunned him for a moment, and renewed the pursuit. As he came up the second time, before he reached me he tried to fire upon me, but as fortune ordered it, his gun missed and left him in a rage. He then rode on, with the weapon raised in his hand, commanding me to stop. I had a round stone in my hand, and when he came near enough, I determined to give him what we used to call a "hard biscuit," and threw the stone, which, from the cry he gave, I knew had hit him somewhere, and caused him to halt until his companion came up with him.

Some may think I did wrong in this, and I am very sure it was very hazardous, for the penalty is very severe upon slaves who strike a white man, but I was after a prize, for which I was willing to risk my life. And I doubt not, any one who reads this, would have done the same. And if it was right for the revolutionary patriots to fight for liberty, it was right for me. . . .

Lucy Delaney

Lucy Delaney was the daughter of a free Illinois woman who had been kidnapped and sold into slavery. When Lucy was twelve, her mother Polly Berry proved her own freedom in a St. Louis court of law. Then, in 1842, she hired a lawyer, Judge Edward Bates, and sued for her daughter Lucy's freedom from a man named Mitchell.

The case took seventeen months to come to trial. During that time, Lucy was held in the St. Louis jail. On the morning when the jury returned its verdict, Lucy sat in court, waiting to hear if she would live her life as a slave or free. Many years later, in 1891, she wrote of that moment in her autobiography, *From the Darkness Cometh the Light, or Struggles for Freedom.*

I had taken my seat in such a condition of helpless terror that I could not tell one person from another. Friends and foes were as one, and vainly did I try to distinguish them. My long confinement, burdened with *harrowing anxiety,* the sleepless night I had just spent, the *unaccountable* absence of my mother, had brought me to an indescribable condition. I felt dazed, as if I were no longer myself. I seemed to be another person—an onlooker—and in my heart dwelt a pity for the poor, lonely girl, with down-cast face, sitting on the bench apart from anyone else in that noisy room. . . .

great uneasiness
unexplainable

Some other business occupied the attention of the Court, and when I had begun to think they had forgotten all about me, Judge Bates arose and said calmly, "Your Honor, I desire to have this girl, Lucy A. Berry, *discharged* before going into any other business."

released

Judge Mullanphy answered "Certainly!" Then the verdict was called for and rendered [and I was granted my freedom] and the jurymen resumed their places. Mr. Mitchell's lawyer jumped up and exclaimed:

"Your Honor, my client demands that this girl be *remanded* to jail. He does not consider that the case has had a fair trial, I am not informed as to what course he intends to pursue, but I am now expressing his present wishes."

returned

Judge Bates was on his feet in a second and cried: "For shame! is it not enough that this girl has been deprived of her liberty for a year and a half, that you must still pursue her after a fair and impartial trial before a jury, in which it was clearly proven and decided that she had every right to freedom? I demand that she be set at liberty at once!"

"I agree with Judge Bates," responded Judge Mullanphy, "and the girl may go!"

Oh! the overflowing thankfulness of my grateful heart at that moment, who could picture it? None but the good God above us!

Harriet Jacobs

Harriet Jacobs escaped from North Carolina with her family, but it took a long time. Afraid to leave her son and daughter behind, Jacobs hid for seven years in her grandmother's attic. Finally, in 1840, her daughter was taken north, and in 1842 Harriet Jacobs made her own escape. A year later, she had her son brought north, and the family was reunited.

$100 REWARD

WILL be given for the apprehension and delivery of my Servant Girl HARRIET. She is a light mulatto, 21 years of age, about 5 feet 4 inches high, of a thick and corpulent habit, having on her head a thick covering of black hair that curls naturally, but which can be easily combed straight. She speaks easily and fluently, and has an agreeable carriage and address. Being a good seamstress, she has been accustomed to dress well, has a variety of very fine clothes, made in the prevailing fashion, and will probably appear, if abroad, tricked out in gay and fashionable finery. As this girl absconded from the plantation of my son without any known cause or provocation, it is probable she designs to transport herself to the North.

The above reward, with all reasonable charges, will be given for apprehending her, or securing her in any prison or jail within the U. States.

All persons are hereby forewarned against harboring or entertaining her, or being in any way instrumental in her escape, under the most rigorous penalties of the law.

JAMES NORCOM.

Edenton, N. C. June 30

After Harriet Jacobs escaped from her master, he offered a reward for her capture. This newspaper advertisement ran three times a week for a two-week period.

Jacobs traveled north by boat, from Edenton, North Carolina, to Philadelphia, with another enslaved woman, Fanny. Jacobs wrote of escaping in her autobiography, in which she called herself "Linda Brent."

When I entered the vessel the captain came forward to meet me. He was an elderly man, with a pleasant *countenance.*   *look*
He showed me to a little box of a cabin, where sat my friend Fanny. She *started* as if she had seen a *spectre.* She gazed on me   *jumped; ghost*
in utter astonishment, and exclaimed, "Linda, can this be [you]? or is it your ghost?" When we were locked in each other's arms, my overwrought feelings could no longer be restrained. My sobs reached the ears of the captain, who came and very kindly reminded us, that for his safety, as well as our own, it would be *prudent* for us not to attract any attention. He said that when   *wise*
there was a sail in sight he wished us to keep below; but at other times, he had no objection to our being on deck. . . .

Fanny and I now talked by ourselves, low and quietly, in our little cabin. She told me of the sufferings she had gone through in making her escape, and of her terrors while she was concealed in her mother's house. Above all, she dwelt on the agony of separation from all her children on that dreadful auction day. She could scarcely *credit* me, when I told her of the place where   *believe*
I had passed nearly seven years. "We have the same sorrows," said I. "No," replied she, "you are going to see your children soon, and there is no hope that I shall ever even hear from mine."

The vessel was soon under way, but we made slow progress. The wind was against us. I should not have cared for this, if we had been out of sight of the town; but until there were miles of water between us and our enemies, we were filled with constant apprehensions that the *constables* would come on board.   *local officials*
Neither could I feel quite at ease with the captain and his men.

I was an entire stranger to that class of people, and I had heard that sailors were rough, and sometimes cruel. We were so completely in their power, that if they were bad men, our situation would be dreadful. Now that the captain was paid for our passage, might he not be tempted to make more money by giving us up to those who claimed us as property? I was naturally *of a confiding disposition,* but slavery had made me suspicious of every body. Fanny did not share my distrust of the captain or his men. She said she was afraid at first, but she had been on board three days while the vessel lay in the dock, and nobody had betrayed her, or treated her otherwise than kindly.

trusting

The captain soon came to advise us to go on deck for fresh air. His friendly and respectful manner, combined with Fanny's testimony, reassured me, and we went with him. He placed us in a comfortable seat, and occasionally entered into conversation. He told us he was a Southerner by birth, and had spent the greater part of his life in the Slave States, and that he had recently lost a brother who traded in slaves. ''But,'' said he, ''it is a *pitiable and degrading* business, and I always felt ashamed to acknowledge my brother in connection with it.'' . . .

sad and shameful

I shall never forget that night. The balmy air of spring was so refreshing! And how shall I describe my sensations when we were fairly sailing on Chesapeake Bay? O, the beautiful sunshine! the exhilarating breeze! and I could enjoy them without fear or restraint. I had never realized what grand things air and sunlight are till I had been deprived of them.

Henry Bibb

Born into slavery in Kentucky in 1815, Henry Bibb first crossed the Ohio River to freedom in 1837, but returned south to rescue his wife and daughter. Recaptured, he escaped again and again, always returning for his family.

He was never able to bring them out of slavery, and in 1840 Henry Bibb finally went north alone to Canada. There he founded a colony for fugitive and free African Americans and began a newspaper, *Voice of the Fugitive.* He sent many of his writings south.

In 1844, Bibb heard from his old Kentucky master, William Gatewood. Gatewood wrote to ask if Henry Bibb the writer was the same Henry Bibb he once owned. Bibb wrote him this letter.

Dear sir:—I am happy to inform you that you are not mistaken in the man whom you sold as property, and received pay for as such. But I thank God that I am not property now, but am regarded as a man like yourself, and although I live far north, I am enjoying a comfortable living by my own *industry.* If you should ever chance to be traveling this way, and will call on me, I will use you better than you did me while you held me as a slave. Think not that I have any *malice* against you, for the cruel treatment which you inflicted on me while I was in your power. As it was the custom of your country, to treat your fellow men as you did me and my little family, I can freely forgive you.

work

ill will

I wish to be remembered in love to my aged mother, and friends; please tell her that if we should never meet again in this life, my prayer shall be to God that we may meet in Heaven, where parting shall be no more.

You wish to be remembered to King and Jack [former slaves]. I am pleased, sir, to inform you that they are both here, well, and doing well. They are both living in Canada West. They are now the owners of better farms than the men are who once owned them.

You may perhaps think hard of us for running away from slavery, but as to myself, I have but one apology to make for it, which is this: I have only to regret that I did not start at an earlier period. I might have been free long before I was. But you had it in your power to have kept me there much longer than you did. I think it is very probable that I should have been a toiling slave on your plantation to-day, if you had treated me differently.

To be *compelled* to stand by and see you whip and slash my wife without mercy, when I could *afford* her no protection, not even by offering myself to suffer the lash in her place, was more than I felt it to be the duty of a slave husband to endure, while the way was open to Canada. My infant child was also frequently flogged by Mrs. Gatewood, for crying, until its skin was bruised literally purple. This kind of treatment was what drove me from home and family, to seek a better home for them. But I am willing to forget the past. I should be pleased to hear from you again, on the reception of this, and should also be very happy to correspond with you often, if it should be agreeable to yourself. I subscribe myself a friend to the oppressed, and Liberty forever.

forced
give

Henry Bibb.

ON TO FREEDOM

The Civil War, which began in 1861, ended the enslavement of four million African Americans. On one side was the Confederacy, eleven southern slaveholding states, fighting to make a separate nation. On the other side was the Union, seventeen free northern states and four slaveholding states, fighting to keep the nation whole.

Many issues divided the Confederate and Union states, but the great dividing issue was slavery. Without that, there would have been no war.

SLAVERY AND WESTWARD EXPANSION

Between 1845 and 1859, the nation expanded its territory all the way west to the Pacific Ocean. Would the new territories be slave or free? Would the dividing line between the free North and the slave South be drawn all the way west? Or would the South become isolated, surrounded on the north and west by free soil?

Southern slaveholders wanted at least some of the new territories to become slave states. Northern abolitionists wanted to abolish slavery everywhere. Others, called Free-Soilers, did not care if the South remained enslaved, as long as the new states were free.

During these years, many attempts were made to keep a balance between slave and free in the new territories. But in 1857, an enslaved man named Dred Scott sued for his freedom, claiming he was a citizen of the free northern half of Missouri. The Supreme Court ruled against Dred Scott. It said that no African American, enslaved or free, could be a citizen of the United States. It also said that slavery was legal in all of the new territories.

The Dred Scott ruling enraged anti-slavery people everywhere. Many called for war. One who did so was John Brown. Brown had fought the extension of slavery into Kansas. Now he raised a small army of men, black and white, to stamp out slavery by force in the South. In 1859, they raided the federal arsenal at Harpers Ferry, Virginia. Brown and many of his men were captured and hanged for treason, but the raid had wide support in the North.

A year after John Brown was hanged, the nation elected an anti-slavery president, Abraham Lincoln. In the two months following Lincoln's inauguration as President, eleven southern states withdrew from the Union and formed their own army. On April 12, 1861, the Confederate forces fired on federal troops at Fort Sumter in South Carolina. The Civil War had begun.

THE EMANCIPATION PROCLAMATION

Unlike many people who were against slavery, Abraham Lincoln was willing to compromise to save the Union. The South could keep its slaves, but there was to be no slavery in the new territories. But

The trial of John Brown as painted by Horace Pippin. Brown was wounded and captured at Harpers Ferry and then brought to trial. Although some wanted him declared insane, he conducted himself with dignity during the trial. When Brown was executed on December 2, 1859, the great American thinker Ralph Waldo Emerson said the convicted fighter would make the place where he was hanged "as glorious as a cross."

in the first two years of the Civil War, Lincoln's Union Army lost as many battles as it won. The Confederate Army used enslaved workers to grow its food, and move its supplies. Lincoln knew that a formal declaration freeing these workers would hurt the Confederate side. So he proposed such a declaration—the Emancipation Proclamation.

On January 1, 1863, the Emancipation Proclamation became law. It made all slaves in the Confederate states "then, thenceforward, and forever free." Many were still held in slavery, but now the war was about their freedom. Each bit of Confederate ground the Union Army won now became free soil.

The Emancipation Proclamation also allowed African Americans, freed and already free, to join the Union Army as soldiers. Almost 200,000 did, helping to bring about the final Union victory in 1865.

Mattie Jackson

The Emancipation Proclamation did not free enslaved people in Missouri, Kentucky, Maryland, or Delaware. These four slaveholding states remained in the Union. The Union Army moved in, and some of the Union soldiers helped the slaves around them. But in these states, and everywhere in the South, the life of enslaved people changed little during the War.

Such was the case for Mattie Jackson and her mother, held in slavery by the Lewis family of St. Louis, Missouri. In her autobiography, *The Story of Mattie J. Jackson,* Mattie wrote of what happened when her mistress learned that the Union Army had taken a nearby Confederate camp.

She then *hastened* to her room with the speed of a deer, nearly ⟶ *ran*
unhinging every door in her flight, replying as she went
that the Niggers and Yankees were seeking to take the country.
One day, after she had visited the kitchen to *superintend* some ⟶ *supervise*
domestic affairs, as she pretended, she became very angry without a word being passed, and said—"I think it has come to a
pretty pass, that old Lincoln, with his long legs, an old rail split- ⟶ *terrible point*
ter, wishes to put the Niggers on an equality with the whites;"
that her children should never be on an equal footing with a
Nigger. She had rather see them dead. As my mother made no
reply to her remarks, she stopped talking, and commenced
venting her spite on my companion servant. On one occasion
Mr. Lewis searched my mother's room and found a picture of
President Lincoln, cut from a newspaper, hanging in her room.
He asked her what she was doing with old Lincoln's picture.
She replied it was there because she liked it. He then knocked
her down three times, and sent her to the *trader's yard* for a ⟶ *stockade*
month as punishment.

Louis Hughes

As the Union Army advanced, slave owners resorted to violence to
keep slaves from crossing the Union lines to freedom. Louis Hughes,
enslaved by the McGee family of Mississippi, remembered what
happened to two men who tried to escape in this way.

Two slaves belonging to one Wallace, one of our nearest
neighbors, had tried to escape to the Union soldiers, but were
caught, brought back and hung. All of our servants were called
up, told every detail of the runaway and capture of the poor
creatures and their shocking murder, and then *compelled* to go ⟶ *forced*
and see them where they hung. I never shall forget the horror

of the scene—it was sickening. The bodies hung at the roadside, where the execution took place, until the blue flies literally swarmed around them, and the *stench* was fearful. This *barbarous* spectacle was for the purpose of showing the passing slaves what would be the fate of those caught in the attempt to escape, and to secure the *circulation* of the details of the awful affair among them, throughout all the neighborhood.

smell; cruel

telling

On April 9, 1865, the South surrendered and the Civil War officially ended, although fighting continued in some places. Some slave owners still refused to let go of their slaves, however, threatening them with death if they tried to flee.

Louis Hughes and a fellow slave, George Washington, escaped from the McGees after the war, but had to leave their wives behind. They found two Union soldiers willing to return with them to the McGee plantation, so they could bring their wives to freedom. In his autobiography, *Thirty Years a Slave*, Louis wrote of the rescue.

After a long and weary ride we reached old Master Jack's a little after sundown. The soldiers rode into the yard ahead of us, and the first person they met was a servant (Frank) at the woodpile. They said to him: "Go in and tell your master, Mr. McGee, to come out, we want to see him," at the same time asking for Louis' and George's wives. . . .

As we drove past them, young McGee went running into the house, saying to his mother: "It is Louis and George, and I'll kill one of them to-night." This raised quite an alarm, and the members of the family told him not to do that, as it would ruin them. As soon as George and I drove up to the first cabin, which was my wife's and Kitty's, we ran in. Kitty met us at the door and said: "I am all ready." She was looking for us. We commenced loading our wagon with our few things. Meanwhile the

soldiers had ridden around a few *rods* and came upon old Mas- *short distance*
ter Jack and the minister of the parish, who were watching as
guards to keep the slaves from running away to the Yankees.
Just think of the outrage upon those poor creatures in forcibly
retaining them in slavery long after the proclamation making
them free had gone into effect beyond all question! As the soldiers rode up to the two men they said: "Hello! what are you
doing here? Why have you not told these two men, Louis and
George, that they are free men—that they can go and come as
they like?" By this time all the family were aroused, and great
excitement prevailed. The soldier's presence drew all the servants near. George and I hurried to fill up our wagon, telling
our wives to get in, as there was no time to lose—we must go
at once. In twenty minutes we were all loaded. My wife, Aunt
Kitty and nine other servants followed the wagon. I waited for
a few moments for Mary Ellen, sister of my wife; and as she
came running out of the white folks' house, she said to her
mistress, Mrs. Farrington: "Good-bye; I wish you good luck."
"I wish you all the bad luck," said she in a rage. But Mary did
not stop to notice her mistress further; and, joining me, we were
soon on the road following the wagon.

Annie L. Burton

In the months following the end of the Civil War, freed African
Americans were on the move everywhere in the South, looking for
lost kin and a better place to live. Many families got back together
at this time.

This was true of Annie L. Burton and her family. She and her
siblings spent the war enslaved on a large Alabama plantation. Their
mother had run away during the war, but when it ended she returned to collect her three children. The family settled in a little hut.

This Theodor Kaufmann painting shows slaves freed by the Union army near the end of the Civil War. Many of the slaves on the move at this time were women and children, since most of the men were taking part in the war on both the North and South sides. The painting's title is "On to Liberty."

They survived on what little food their mother managed to scavenge. Many years later, in her autobiography, *Memories of Childhood's Slavery Days,* Annie L. Burton wrote of what happened to the family one cold, rainy night.

All at once there came a knock at the door. My mother answered the knock. When she opened the door, there stood a white woman and three little children, all dripping with the rain. My mother said, "In the name of the Lord, where are you going on such a night, with these children?" The woman said, "Auntie, I am travelling. Will you please let me stop here to-night, out of the rain, with my children?" My mother said, "Yes, honey. I ain't got much, but what I have got I will share with you." "God bless you!" They all came in. We children looked in wonder at what had come. But my mother scattered her own little brood and made a place for the *forlorn* wanderers. She said, "Wait, honey, let me turn over that *hoe* cake." Then the two women fell to talking, each telling a tale of woe. After a time, my mother called out, "Here, you, Louise, or some one of you, put some *fagots* under the pot, so these *pease* can get done." We couldn't put them under fast enough, first one and then another of us children, the mothers still talking. Soon my mother said, "Draw that hoe cake one side, I guess it is done." My mother said to the woman, "Honey, ain't you got no husband?" She said, "No, my husband got killed in the war." My mother replied, "Well, my husband died right after the war. I have been away from my little brood for four years. With a hard struggle, I have got them away from the Farrin plantation, for they did not want to let them go. But I got them. I was determined to have them. But they would not let me have them if they could have kept them. With God's help I will keep them from starving. The white folks are good to me. They give me work, and I know, with God's help, I can get along." The white woman replied, "Yes, Auntie, my husband left me on a rich man's plantation. This man promised to look out for me until my husband came home; but he got killed in the war, and the Yankees have set his negroes free and he said he could not help me any more, and we would have to do the best we could for ourselves. I gave my things to a woman to keep for me until I could find my

sad

cornmeal

sticks; peas

kinsfolk. They live about fifty miles from here, up in the country.   *family*
I am on my way there now." My mother said, "How long will
it take you to get there?" "About three days, if it don't rain."
My mother said, "Ain't you got some way to ride there?" "No,
Auntie, there is no way of riding up where my folks live, the
place where I am from."

We hoped the talk was most ended, for we were anxiously
watching that pot. Pretty soon my mother seemed to realize our
existence. She exclaimed, "My Lord! I suppose the little children are nearly starved. Are those pease done, young ones?"
She turned and said to the white woman, "Have you-all had
anything to eat?" "We stopped at a house about dinner time,
but the woman didn't have anything but some bread and but-
termilk." My mother said, "Well, honey, I ain't got but a little,
but I will divide with you." The woman said, "Thank you, Auntie.
You just give my children a little; I can do without it."

Then came the dividing. We all watched with all our eyes to
see what the shares would be. My mother broke a mouthful of
bread and put it on each of the tin plates. Then she took the old
spoon and equally divided the pea soup. We children were seated
around the fire, with some little wooden spoons. But the wooden
spoons didn't quite go round, and some of us had to eat with
our fingers. Our share of the meal, however, was so small that
we were as hungry when we finished as when we began.

My mother said, "Take that rag and wipe your face and hands,
and give it to the others and let them use it, too. Put those plates
upon the table." We immediately obeyed orders, and took our
seats again around the fire. "One of you go and pull that straw
out of the corner and get ready to go to bed." We all lay down
on the straw, the white children with us, and my mother covered us over with the blanket. We were soon in the "Land of
Nod," forgetting our empty stomachs. The two mothers still

continued to talk, sitting down on the only seats, a couple of blocks. A little back against the wall my mother and the white woman slept.

Bright and early in the morning we were called up, and the rest of the hoe cake was eaten for breakfast, with a little meat, some coffee sweetened with molasses. The little wanderers and their mother shared our meal, and then they started again on their journey towards their home among their kinsfolk, and we never saw them again.

FINAL WORDS

The writers whose words are collected in this book have inspired others to reimagine slavery and create new stories of courage, love, and loss. One such person is Rita Dove, whose poem, *Someone's Blood*, tells of the parting of an enslaved mother and child.

> I stood at 6 a.m. on the wharf,
> thinking: *This is Independence, Missouri.*
> *I am to stay here. The boat goes on to New Orleans.*
> My life seemed minutes old, and here it was ending.
>
> I was silent, although she clasped me
> and asked forgiveness for giving me life.
> As the sun broke the water into a thousand needles
> tipped with the blood from someone's finger,
>
> the boat came gently apart from the wharf.
> I watched till her face could not distinguish itself
> from that shadow floated on broken sunlight.
> I stood there. I could not help her. I forgive.

SOURCES

Bibb, Henry. *Narrative of the Life and Adventures of Henry Bibb, an American Slave. Written by Himself.* In Gilbert Osofsky, editor, *Puttin' on Ole Massa: The Slave Narratives of Henry Bibb, William Wells Brown, and Solomon Northup.* New York: Harper & Row, 1969.

Burton, Annie L. *Memories of Childhood's Slavery Days.* Reprinted in William Andrews, editor, *Six Women's Slave Narratives.* New York: Oxford University Press, 1988.

Cornelia. "My Mother Was The Smartest Black Woman In Eden." In *Unwritten History of Slavery: Autobiographical Accounts of Negro Ex-Slaves.* Washington D.C.: Microcard Editions, 1968. Reprinted here by permission of Fisk University Library.

Delaney, Lucy. *From the Darkness Cometh the Light, or Struggles for Freedom.* Reprinted in William Andrews, editor, *Six Women's Slave Narratives.* New York: Oxford University Press, 1988.

Douglass, Frederick. *Narrative of the Life of Frederick Douglass, an American Slave. Written by Himself.* New York: Penguin Books, 1982.

Douglass, Frederick. *My Bondage and My Freedom.* Urbana and Chicago: University of Illinois Press, 1987.

Dove, Rita. "Someone's Blood." From *The Yellow House on the Corner,* by Rita Dove. Pittsburgh: Carnegie Mellon University Press, 1989. Reprinted by permission of the author.

Elizabeth. *Memoir of Old Elizabeth, A Coloured Woman.* Reprinted in William Andrews, editor, *Six Women's Slave Narratives.* New York: Oxford University Press, 1988.

Equiano, Olaudah. *The Interesting Narratives of the Life of Olaudah Equiano, or Gustavus Vassa, the African, written by Himself.* In Arna Bontemps, editor, *Great Slave Narratives.* Boston: Beacon Press, 1969.

Hughes, Louis. *Thirty Years a Slave, From Bondage to Freedom. The Institution of Slavery as seen on the Plantation and in the Home of the Planter.* Reprint. Detroit: Negro History Press, 1969.

Jackson, Andrew. *Narrative and Writings of Andrew Jackson, of Kentucky.* Reprint. Miami: Mnemosyne Publishing, 1969.

Jackson, Mattie J. *The Story of Mattie J. Jackson.* Reprinted in William Andrews, editor, *Six Women's Slave Narratives.* New York: Oxford University Press, 1988.

Jacobs, Harriet. *Incidents in the Life of a Slave Girl. Written by Herself.* Cambridge, Massachusetts: Harvard University Press, 1987.

Northup, Solomon. *Twelve Years a Slave.* Baton Rouge and London: Louisiana State University Press, 1968.

Pennington, James W. C. *The Fugitive Blacksmith.* In Arna Bontemps, editor, *Great Slave Narratives.* Boston: Beacon Press, 1969.

Prince, Mary. *The History of Mary Prince, a West Indian Slave, Related by Herself*. Reprinted in William Andrews, editor, *Six Women's Slave Narratives*. New York: Oxford University Press, 1988.

Scriven, Abream. Letter to Dinah Jones. From Charles Colcock Jones Papers, Manuscript Department, Howard-Tilton Memorial Library, Tulane University, New Orleans, Louisiana 70118-5682. Reprinted by permission.

FURTHER READING

Berry, James. *Ajeemah & His Son.* New York: HarperCollins, 1992.

Davis, Ossie. *Escape to Freedom: A Play about Young Frederick Douglass.* New York: Puffin Books, 1990.

Goldman, Martin S. *Nat Turner and the Southampton Revolt of 1831.* New York: Franklin Watts, 1992.

Hamilton, Virginia. *Many Thousand Gone: African-Americans from Slavery to Freedom.* New York: Knopf, 1993.

Lester, Julius. *This Strange New Feeling.* New York: Scholastic, 1985.

———. *To Be a Slave.* New York: Dial, 1968.

Levine, Ellen. *If You Traveled on the Underground Railroad.* New York: Scholastic, 1993.

McKissack, Patricia, and Fredrick McKissack. *Frederick Douglass: The Black Lion.* Chicago: Childrens Press, 1987.

Meltzer, Milton. *All Times, All Peoples: A World History of Slavery.* New York: HarperCollins, 1980.

Northup, Solomon. *Twelve Years a Slave, Eighteen Forty-One to Eighteen Fifty-Three.* Retold by W. A. Dean. Bossier City, LA: Everett, 1990.

Ofosu-Appiah, L. H. *People in Bondage: African Slavery in the Modern Era.* Minneapolis: Lerner, 1992.

Petry, Ann. *Harriet Tubman: Conductor on the Underground Railroad.* New York: HarperCollins, 1955.

———. *Tituba of Salem Village.* New York: HarperCollins, 1992.

Rappaport, Doreen. *Escape from Slavery: Five Journeys to Freedom.* New York: HarperCollins, 1991.

INDEX

❈

ABOUT THE AUTHOR

Michele Stepto is a lecturer in English and
American Studies at Yale University, where
she has taught courses on children's literature
and the literature of slavery. She has written
on Frederick Douglass and other American
authors, and has published a book for young
readers, *Snuggle Piggy and the Magic Blanket*.